Fast Track to Peace

Applying 'A Course in Miracles'

Bette Jean Cundiff

Fast Track to Peace

Copyright 2018
Bette Jean Cundiff

ALL RIGHTS RESERVED

Miracle Experiences and You Publishing

bettejeancundiff.blogspot.com

ISBN: 9798680303474

Fast Track to Peace

A few thoughts before you start . . .

Are you struggling with anything at all? Well then, this is for you. Take the time honored healing offered by the spiritual psychology of the world renowned *"A Course in Miracles"*, and add the insight and humor of acclaimed author Bette Jean Cundiff and gain the tools to handle the pesky ego for the rest of your life.

Whether you are reading this in book form or following along as an online mini course, each section is concise, easy to understand and will challenge you to look within and make changes. Take your time as you read, study and explore, then contemplate the questions offered in each section. They are deceptively simple but stuffed with wisdom.

Fast Track to Peace

Here is a powerful overview of the ego and the process of correction An excellent beginning for a newbie in spiritual studies, or a turbo charge for the student already studying for years.

You can study this as a private discipline or you can get together with a family member or a group of friends and follow along as a study group. Private study offers person contemplation. Group study offers lively, insightful discussion. Either is an excellent approach.

Start now, and Fast Track to Peace.

Fast Track to Peace

Your Personal Reality Game

Your mission, should you wish to accept it, is to navigate through life successfully.

You will be given a finite but unknown number of challenges.

Fast Track to Peace

You will be given the following tools to use as you choose:

1. your body with its many possibilities as well as limitations
2. your mind with its ability to imagine and to worry
3. your emotions, deep and dangerous.

All three tools can be powerful engines for success or disaster – use them judiciously.

Fast Track to Peace

Your challenges will be in the following three areas:

1. health

2. wealth

3. relationships

Fast Track to Peace

Your most insidious foe will come in three disguises:

😯 1. the belief you are separate and different from all others – this will bring intense fear

☹️ 2. the belief you are unworthy – this is marked by debilitating guilt

😠 3. the need to find fault and redirect blame away from yourself – anger, rage, concealment through righteous indignation and a sense of superiority are its hallmarks.

Fast Track to Peace

Your game will take you on a spiraling climb through levels of challenges. Success will be marked by a sense of wellbeing in each area of your life.

Your secret weapon as a Reality Game Team member can be found within you and is the ability to connect with all aspects of life – people, nature and the universe at large.

♥

Unfortunately, to use this secret weapon you must discover where it is hidden, how to access it successfully on a need to use basis, and to use it with discretion and wisdom.

Fast Track to Peace

Your reward for success will be a deep peace that permeates all areas of your existence and is a treasure house of an unlimited source of contentment. All fear, guilt and anger will disappear and only love and upliftment will remain.

Should you not be able to complete all your challenges successfully within your allotted time period, you will be given another opportunity to enter the game once more in another lifetime. But, be aware, though the basic components of the game will be the same, major areas will be camouflaged and seem completely different, alien and perhaps more difficult for each new game you enter.

Fast Track to Peace

Choose carefully!

Play well and nobly.

Your life depends on it!

Fast Track to Peace

Fast Track to Peace

PART I

All About Ego

And

Ego's evil offspring

Guilt, Fear and Anger

Fast Track to Peace

Ego, for better or worse

Are you walking around in a body? Then you have an ego in working order. Egos run our lives, our bodies, our developing lifestyles. Egos are praised and egos are cursed – they are either necessary for proper psychological development, or an evil that drives us into becoming self centered bores or even sociopaths.

But, the most important thing to remember about egos is that we all have one, with its unlikable offspring guilt, fear, and anger. What we do with our egos and their offspring, for better or worse is what this book is about.

'Jekyl and Hyde' might be a good name for ego, but for now I prefer going with the simple nomenclature – Survivor.

Here is your brain honed down to its simplest directive - use all its expansive resources to keep your body alive. Alive is good. Dead is bad. Anything that in the slightest bit resembles death, dying and loss is bad.

Every physical sense, every synapse lining up to connect electrical pathways, all the information you collect, all the habits you form, all of this is designed to keep you alive. And to survive you must keep pushing yourself to your highest level of performance. Whether it is the most daring athlete, the richest financial genius, or just going for the gold in resident couch potato – your brain, the working arm of your ego wants you, no needs you, to survive at what it has deemed 'the best for you'.

The good part of ego is that it will direct you to get better at what it deems important for your survival. The bad part is that it can collect mistaken beliefs about certain things being helpful when they are really hurtful – Jekyl and Hyde at odds – and at your expense.

Ultimately, by following these stepping stones, we cannot but come to the conclusion that keeping this corpse walking around forever is a really rotten idea. (Sorry, I couldn't resist the pun.)

Providentially, our egos will guide us to do anything to survive, so we can teach our mind to guide it to what true living is. We can teach ourselves that the body is

Fast Track to Peace

only a tool to help us gain life, and life is so much more than just living in a body. Then we can take that quantum leap across miraculous boundaries using our egos to fling us into the arms of Something indescribable and all encompassing.

Before, we go to that most important first step we must shine a light on ego's offspring – the emotions of guilt, fear and anger – the wolf pack lurking within.

important point

"Providentially, our egos will guide us to do anything
to survive,
so we can teach it what true living is."

Fast Track to Peace

Thoughts, Suggestions, Things to Practice

Signs that ego is at work will be feelings of guilt, fear and anger. Since we are so used to ignoring these feelings, and/or calling them by other more acceptable names, why not make a list of other emotions that fall into these three categories so you will notice ego's shenanigans easily.

For instance:
1. Guilt – can feel like unworthiness
    a. (What else may be a disguise of guilt?)
2. Fear – can feel like anxiety
    a. (What else may be a disguise of fear?)
3. Anger – can feel like righteous indignation
    a. (What else may be a disguise for anger?)

Fast Track to Peace

Let's meet

The Evil Triplets

Fast Track to Peace

Guilt

Your Inner Wolf

Howling an ululating poem to the moon, a lone wolf is silhouetted against the night sky. He turns, notices you watching and haughtily leaves to return to his pack. How majestic! How powerful! Chills run down your spine as you observe the primal drama. Oh, to be a wolf and to share in that majesty and power yourself.

Over eons wolves have developed an unerring dynamic for survival called the pack. With the pack the wolf lives, and without it he or she dies. That same instinct for successfully living in society is tied in a strangle hold to our instinct to keep our bodies going. Within wolf or human, ego strives to perfect living in a pack. So, many of the same survival tools for wolves have been honed by human society as well. And those very same tactics that are richly alluring in their romance and strength in the wolf are often addictive, destructive and sinister in humans. Let's

Fast Track to Peace

look at why something that works so perfectly in the animal kingdom falls flat on its face for people.

Now, I am no expert on wolves, I've simply watched those same nature shows you have on TV. But, one thing stands out – to keep the pack in working order misconduct is reprimanded quickly and fiercely. If you don't keep the rules you endanger the survival of the pack. Just watch your pet dog. Once you establish yourself as alpha in his pack, your word is law. As your pet scoffs up that left over piece of pizza on the coffee table, you raise your voice slightly, and he stops, the ears go down and he droops off with a distinctly guilty slouch.

Guilt is a tool: Make the pack member feel guilty and the miscreant usually stops. If that's not enough, fierceness can turn to viciousness and even a ripping out of the throat, a sure way of ending wrong actions, permanently, and keeping the pack safe.

Guilt is a tool to keep others in line. Now, this is really great in a wolf pack when long logical discussions are severely limited. But, humans have hopefully evolved to, rarely, if ever ripping out a youngster's throat for taking the car keys when he shouldn't. Though sometimes a few family gatherings I have observed in the past, thankfully not mine, and seen from afar, can emotionally feel just like that.

However, guilt is still used as an extremely potent tool for keeping people around you in line. You use it on them and they on you. Some examples: Your mother calls, starts asking about your job, your friends, why you don't call more often, and suddenly you feel like you are five years old again and you start to droop and want to creep away in a distinctly guilty slouch. Or, your spouse comes in later than usual for dinner and you ask with arched eyebrow, "So where have you been?" The atmosphere immediately turns grim.

So, what does *A Course in Miracles* say about guilt and its sidekicks anger and fear? Well, these emotions may occur, but holding onto them for longer than a moment to recognize them is 'unjustified'. What does this mean? We are human, part of the animal branch on the tree of life and all emotions will flow through us at one time or another. However, when we hold onto guilt, anger and the resultant fear, replaying it again and again in our minds, we are changing the original law of the pack into a human dysfunction. Our ego has gained reinforcement that this is good, when in fact it is slowly killing us.

Fast Track to Peace

There are deeper and darker areas of guilt within us the ego keeps carefully locked away. When unworthiness from childhood is reinforced by the world around us damage begins to erode our subconscious leaving it tragically leprous. Ego began a massive campaign to hide these feelings of guilt, fear and unexpressed anger in a stupendously misguided campaign of coping mechanisms . For now, though, we need not label the myriad array of neuroses and psychoses .

All we actually need to do is recognize that guilt is neither good nor bad, after all. Guilt is simply a red flag suggesting we may have done something incorrectly. All we need do next is assess if our actions need to change. If they do, then suck it up and change. If we assess our actions as O.K. then we can go about our business as usual. Not to worry. How to assess correctly the one or the other will be reviewed in later sections.

The glory and majesty of the pack seen on a distant snow encrusted hill is working just perfectly. They know what they are doing. Guilt, fear and a short burst of anger keeps the pack vibrant and functioning. Just remember, however, when we feel ourselves wallowing in unworthiness and wanting to dump that extra dollop of guilt and anger onto another, assess what we are doing very carefully by asking for the insight and direction of the your inner power. And when that glob of guilt smacks you in the face, shake it off, change if you need to and move right along. That's the sign of being human and humanity becomes just as glorious and majestic as the primal wolf pack.

But for now, listen carefully. If you do, you will hear the echo of human laughter and the ululating song of the wolf echoing together. Their songs ring through the valleys and across the distant mountains in a joyous serenade of love.

important point

When we hold onto guilt, anger and the resultant fear, replaying it again and again in our minds, we are changing the original law of the pack into a human dysfunction.

Fast Track to Peace

Thoughts, Suggestions, Things to Practice

1. Notice how and when others dump guilt on you.

2. Notice how and when YOU dump guilt on others.

3. Now try to find the reason you all are trying to control others with guilt.

Take heart, this is just the beginning of the correction process.

FEAR

HIGH ANXIETY

Have you ever noticed first thing in the morning, before you even start thinking about anything, you already feel a twinge of anxiety? Oh boy! Your day hasn't even begun, and you are already worried about 'it'.

What is the 'it'? Well, it is actually anything you decide it will be. This is the concern that you may have done, are doing or will do something wrong, and fear the consequences. Let me explain.

Fear, by any other name is still fear, one of the offspring of ego – another one of its survival tools like guilt and anger. If you want to survive you need to be constantly vigilant. And that constant vigilance is fear, anxiety and an underlying, nagging sense of unease and foreboding. Recognize that same old feeling? Sure you do. We all do.

Fast Track to Peace

Just like its sibling guilt and its constantly underlying feeling of unworthiness, which we reviewed in the last section, fear can be another incredible helper. Without fear you would say, "Hi, kitty," to the roaring saber tooth tiger looming in front of you. Or, nonchalantly cross an L.A. freeway at rush hour as you twitter away on your cell phone. Or, how about mentioning to your wife how that dress really does make her look fat? Now, that's a really scary thing you should avoid.

Yes, fear can be helpful, so we can recognize danger signs and take the necessary steps for survival.

But, what happens when fear is unchecked, runs rampant and erodes our subconscious? We become deeply incapacitated and emotionally paralyzed. This fear can run the gamut from becoming tongue tied when that perfect someone steps up to you and says, "Hi". To being unable to leave your house because you believe aliens from space are lurking outside your door and you make all your family wear tin foil hats.

So, what to do about ego's second offspring, fear?

When you feel that old anxiety starts to build, take a sweet, deep breath. Focus on your immediate environment. Feel the air on your skin and the tactile sense of the chair you may be sitting on. Close your eyes and ask your inner knowing Self, "Is there anything I should be concerned about right this moment?"

Now, listen quietly and should any specific concern occur to you. Ask, "What is the most helpful, peaceful action I should take right now?" Then, listen once more. Remember, the peaceful, helpful answer always makes you feel peaceful! The right answer always gives you a sense of, "Of course. Now I know just what to do." It feels right, and gives you a sense of O.K.ness.

Anxiety, like guilt is a built in mechanism, but we can learn to recognize it before it becomes that huge monster in the closet. We can do something corrective – Ask for insight and follow the peaceful answer. Just a little training and practice will bring life gently back into a safe perspective.

important point

Anxiety, like guilt is a built in mechanism, but we can learn to recognize it before it becomes that huge monster in the closet.

Thoughts, Suggestions, Things to Practice

How is fear affecting your life?

1. Take time to list or even start journaling all the issues and times during the day or week that anxiety grabs you by the throat, gives you an upset stomach, sends you to the wine bottle or the extra sleep aid at night. Then ask for peaceful assurance.

Try not to become overwhelmed when you notice how often this happens and how it is handicapping you. Breathe. Ask for assurance, and go on to the next section.

ANGER

CONTROL AT ALL COST

Righteous indignation! Another name for anger all prettied up and looking super respectable. Here we have the last of ego's offspring, the sibling to guilt and fear. The warrior part of the terrible triplets. Anger.

Guilt and fear are debilitating and hamstring us emotionally and physically. They tie us up in knots, drag us back into bed to pull the cover up and over. They keep us from not just engaging in life, but from enjoying life.

But, anger, now there's the 'man!' Here's the action guy, the badass, the knight in shining armor. Anger rises up and unleashed saves your sorry self. Oh, boy, that feels gooooood!

But, does it really? Let's take a peek at what's really happening to us when we let the monster out of the bag.

Fast Track to Peace

When we pull those covers up and over because of guilt and fear we are actually feeling that everything is out of our control. We are now the ultimate victim. Everything happens to us. Nobody understands us. No one loves us. The world treats us like garbage. Ignores us. Rules our lives. Pushes us around. Disses us!

We aint got no respect!

And as we lay there in bed, something ugly and insidious begins to uncurl deep inside. A spark leads to a flame to a raging inferno. Anger has awakened.

How DARE they do that to ME!!!!!

The beast with dragon's tail and flaming tongue roars from your innards and now – YOU ARE IN CONTROL!

First you spend delicious hours thinking of the justification for your thoughts and actions. Then more hours hunkering down with frown and surly looks as you plan your revenge.

And when everything is in place (and of course this whole process might unfold in the blink of an eye) you attack. Maybe subtle, nasty sarcasm will snake out to bite your victim. Maybe a sour scowl will be sufficient. Ha! You'll show them. Or, maybe a full out frontal assault of

Fast Track to Peace

words and fists will bring you what you want most – control!

Your first two siblings are inwardly painful, but anger is ACTION. Even when you are only thinking about your anger, you have a mistaken belief that you are actually doing something corrective. If only in your own mind you are proving to yourself that you are the victim, the innocent party. You no longer need to feel guilt and the fear of retribution. You are the one that is in the right. Your anger is now that prettied up righteous indignation. They're wrong and you are right. So there!

But, what a price we pay for needing to find everyone else wrong so we can feel guilt free. Anger eats us up alive. Raises our blood pressure, sends gastric juices to burn up stomach and esophagus. And that's just the most obvious result. What is not obvious to us but unmistakable to others is how unpleasant we are. No one wants to be near us. After all, closeness to us might be dangerous to another's health and well being.

What to do? Just like the first two survival techniques that go viral in our subconscious we need to STOP. Breath and here is the hard part, be willing to be wrong in our assessment of the situation. Yes, I know admitting we are wrong is fundamentally abhorrent to the ego. But, if we allow that peaceful inner Voice to show us something else, we will be miraculously surprised.

Now, we have insight into our preciousness, our safety and our sacredness. And what is really important, we are able to see others with compassion. We see their egos are running them into the ground. We understand their fears, their sense of unworthiness and we feel sorry for them.

And miraculous of all, we not only lose our anger, but we actually want to help them.

In the wolf pack, anger is a quick flare up to nudge a pup back into right behavior for the safety of the pack. And then it is gone. No harm, no foul. So, when you feel that anger begin to rise ask for that different, miraculous perspective. Then you will feel your own strength grow into a beautifully magnanimousness flow.

important point

What to do? Just like the first two survival techniques that go viral in our subconscious we need to STOP. Breath and here is the hard part, be willing to be wrong in our assessment of the situation.

Fast Track to Peace

Thoughts, Suggestions, Things to Practice

This may be a little hard to do:

1. Remember the last argument you had when you felt really justified in telling that person off (or maybe punching their lights out). Now, take a deep breath and see if you can recognize the evil triplets at work in yourself and the other person. If this is too hard, at least remind yourself that anger is hurting you.

This takes a lot of willingness and guts but remember, no one has to know what you are trying to do. (At least not yet) And the payoff will be huge!

Fast Track to Peace

Part II

Taking the Fast Track

The Starting Line

From your first breath you are making decisions about your happiness. Not getting what you want? Scream bloody murder! And usually your needs are met pretty quick. Happiness is accomplished easily because not too many decisions need be made at this point. However, as time goes on and years pass, life becomes more complex than having Mom or Dad fill that empty tummy and change the wet, smelly diaper. An insidious new complication slinks into your life to stay there until your die – people.

You will need to learn how to deal with the sibling who gets Mom's attention, the kids in the sandbox who grab your toys, the students who turn their back on you in the school yard. You have stepped up to the starting line of life - learning to get along socially.

But wait. Ego has sent along its evil offspring, the triplets of guilt, fear and anger to help you cope. This the

Fast Track to Peace

time when you start building habits of a lifetime. You discover this huge vacant hole in your subconscious and begin filling it with emotional experiences that will determine your happiness quotient for decades to come. And ego is just loving this opportunity to 'help' you.

Rest assured, if you are reading these words you have already stuffed your subconscious with a huge amount of garbage. True, some of it is good, but most of it is the monumental landfill of a lifetime, right inside you. And it's pretty spooky in there. Many a night your dreams have been invaded by alien forces from the dark side – your own emotions molded by ego and the evil triplets into monsters.

Not to worry. That's why you have chosen to read these words and clean up your inner environment. And you will. You are just getting started. (Well, maybe you have been in training to fast track to peace using other excellent sources. Great. Keep at it. This will be one more turbo boost to keep you moving along.)

So, let's start with the right equipment for the clean-up – a shovel. This one will seem a little unwieldy but you will get ample opportunity to practice with it. The slogan on its handle says,

Fast Track to Peace

"Would you rather be right, or happy". Translation? Are you willing to be wrong!

I can feel you bristle at that. "What", you demand. "Wrong? Why do I need to be wrong?" Your voice rising in a minor shriek as you ask. "I'm here to feel good about myself, not bad!"

Good point. But, you may need to review the first sections again on ego to understand why being right all the time is ego's golden rule on getting along in society. Remember, ego points out that if you are in the right then you are the innocent party and someone else (maybe everyone else) is wrong and they will get the wrath of the righteous. Being right places you in the top dog position on righteousness.

Within your subconscious the last thing you want to be is guilty and unworthy since that will make you a target for attack. And that is what makes you really feel bad! So, grab the shovel and prepare to clean up your very own 'Super Fund Site". This is the first tentative step toward learning true innocence – willingness to be wrong. Start shoveling.

Fast Track to Peace

important point

Remember, ego points out that if you are in the right then you are the innocent party and someone else (maybe everyone else) is wrong. This places you in the top dog position.

Fast Track to Peace

Thoughts, Suggestions, Things to Practice

1. Notice how people, including yourself, use 'in your face' arguments to prove they are right, and therefore top dog.

2. Since trying to be right by arguing your point all the time is exhausting. Try using this reminder each time you need to prove something. "I would rather be **happy** than right." And let the argument go.

3. Before you go to bed each night, repeat this phrase ten time, "I am beginning to clean up my subconscious and it feels so good."

Fast Track to Peace

Who's looking at me?

Have you ever had the experience of not really noticing yourself fully when you look in the mirror regularly each day? I sort of glance quickly as I go by just to make sure nothing is drastically out of place. Or I put on my makeup with my reflection blown way up so I can get the eyeliner straight, but never look at my face as a whole.

Then every once in awhile . . .BLAM! I stop and stare and wonder who the heck that old lady is that's staring back at me. I was sure she was a lot younger the last time I looked. What a rude awakening! Well, if we take an honest look at ourselves and our thoughts and behaviors, what would we really find? That's what this next step is about. It's time for a rude awakening. And it ain't always pretty.

Chameleons are cool little things, changing their colors to blend with their environment. But it just isn't cool when you are an adult and it's time to get real. We have tried so hard to be what we think others want or need us to be we have lost the real us as we change with each encounter. We are always trying to survive by being something, well, anything, that can get us through the day - the job interview, the family gathering, the luncheon or dinner party, or going on that first date.

At the end of the day we review our encounters adding new lofty dialogue, meaty phrases that now can win the arguments, and we convince ourselves that the losses and humiliations were actually stupendous wins. We were great! This tactic may make us feel better, but never allows us to own up to our mistakes and pretentiousness so we can correct them in the future. Or, we emotionally revel in guilt and unworthiness and beat ourselves up in emotional and sometimes physical ways as we hate ourselves. Yuk! This tactic keeps us stuck and miserable. Ego loves misery and dishonesty.

Being honest with ourselves is hard work. Mainly because ego will work even harder to hide, camouflage and stuff down anything that threatens its Machiavellian logic. Yet, accepting that we are wrong is that first piece of equipment to clean up our inner dump site. Yes, suck it up! We have to be able to admit we are wrong and accept that

Fast Track to Peace

we are not perfect in this world. It's uncomfortable and necessary. Sort of like dumpster diving.

Remember, that everyone else is being just as dishonest about themselves. Yup, they like you have crafted cardboard cutouts of who they want to be at any given time. At work, it's the competent cutout. At home with the kids, it's the playmate or the stern rule maker. And that takes two different cutouts. But, wait there's more! At every social encounter we are rushing to create new cutouts of ourselves to fit the people and encounters. Whew! It's hard to keep track.

Just think about it. You are holding cutouts in front of yourself all the time. And other people are holding cutouts in front of them all the time. And now it gets really squirrely. You are making a cutout for the other person of what you believe they are and seeing that. They are putting one in front of you based on their belief about you. Now you have layers of cutouts like walls hiding the real selves from each other.

So, is anybody actually talking to anybody else? Well, no! Layers of cutouts are saying things, but they are saying it into a void. The real meaning is hidden behind the walls.

Fast Track to Peace

Kind of makes you understand why communication breaks down so easily.

Ha haaa! Now we are down to the next layer of garbage in the landfill. What is true communication if we don't understand our true selves and neither does anyone else? Grab on, this is your next special shovel entitled:

Everyone is either calling desperately for help, or offering help in the only way they know how

Recognizing this as the essence of any communication will be the dynamite that breaks down the glued together detritus of decades.

Here is a personal example:

My father was a Captain in the New York City Fire Department. His nickname was 'by the book Buchanan'. He believed in rules and followed his religion accordingly. After I started studying 'A Course in Miracles' a career opened for me traveling to 'Course' groups around the country giving lectures. My father just couldn't handle it.

Fast Track to Peace

He felt I should be an at home mother, plus the liberal and unusual teaching of the 'Course' seemed offensive to him. He approached me one day, loomed over me and stated, "You just keep going downhill!"

At that moment, as I looked up at him, all the teaching about loving communication filled my mind and without editing I replied gently, "I know we don't agree on all of this and maybe never will, but I know you are saying this because you love me. And I love you for it."

His eyes filled with tears, he smiled sweetly, patted me on the shoulder and walked away.

In this example, at that moment I saw him as the loving father he was, beneath the stern cutout, and he saw me as his beloved child loving him back. That's how true communication works. I saw him both calling for love and trying to help me, both at the same time.

So, we can and will find spiritual perfection behind the cutouts and underneath all the garbage. Start slowly by observing what you are saying and doing. It's OK if don't yet know how to change, but it is absolutely necessary that you want something different. You want peace.

Fast Track to Peace

(Pssst... it's OK to keep working on the following chapters even if you don't think you have 'completed' this one fully. You are moving more quickly along the fast track even if you don't realize it yet.)

important point

Everyone is either calling desperately for help, or offering help in the only way they know how.

Fast Track to Peace

Thoughts, Suggestions, Things to Practice

1. Take some time to contemplate who you have needed to be, the cutouts you have made of yourself and others in your daily encounters.

2. Using your watch or phone as a prompt, remind yourself every fifteen or thirty minutes to review the day's encounters and communications.

3. Note if you and they have been calling for help or offering help, no matter the words used.

Using the 'F' Word

Have you ever heard someone say, "Yes, I will forgive you, but I will never forget!" Just so you know, that ain't forgiveness. How about the gritted teeth, "Yes, I will forgive you, but don't ever do that again!" Nope, that's not forgiveness either.

Time to take a good look at that uncomfortable 'F' word and discover what true forgiveness actually is and how it really works. This will be your third shovel for dredging up and then releasing that garbage down inside your psyche.

Remember this: You can never forgive when you see the unforgivable as, well, unforgivable. And you may have some truly painful and ugly unforgivable memories

Fast Track to Peace

stuffed in the back closet of your mind. Your past is probably littered with incidents that have been devastating.

From child abuse, to humiliations, to ostracization by loved ones, betrayals from people as well as your own body that has seemed to betray you with disabilities, and then there's war, famine, poverty, death of the innocent and young - all crushing your sense of worth, bringing unbelievable grief and anger. Some horrors have been forced on you and others you have forced on yourself. How can you even think about forgiving these atrocities and the persons who have caused them? Let's face it you hate them and you hate yourself.

O.K. That's a little dark, but there is hope. When true forgiveness releases your mind and heart it will be, well, a miracle. So, let's take some time to understand how your mind works and how to make it work for you rather than against you.

Picture your mind shaped like a pyramid. Not your physical brain, but your mind which is so much more.

Fast Track to Peace

```
          /\
         /  \
Conscious Mind
       /_____\
      /        \
Subconscious
    /_____\
   /              \
Super Conscious
  /                \
 /_____\
```

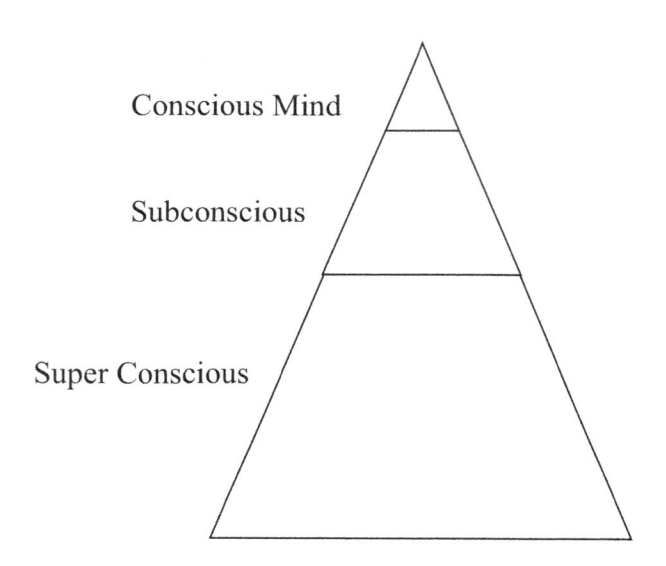

In this super simple illustration notice the pyramid, aka your mind, is divided into three parts.

Notice the top part, consciousness is the smallest. Here you make the everyday decisions like drinking coffee regular or decaf, finishing the report now or later, diet or not to diet, etc. These are done almost on automatic.

The middle part, your subconscious is next in size. In here lurks the good, the bad and the ugly. Your memories and your habits that run your automatic decisions

Fast Track to Peace

are stored here. Here encamped are the evil offspring of ego – guilt, fear, anger. Behold the ego's kingdom. Dark, bitter, fueled with hate. And yes, a few glorious bright parts. Unfortunately, vastly outnumbered by the sludge.

And the last third, what we could call Super Consciousness is actually endless without a true bottom at all for it opens to the whole of Creation filled with the Love of the Universe. Here lies the realm of Light. And notice I do use capital letters purposefully when I refer to this realm within you.

When you make the decision to change, you activate the top part, your conscious mind. But, uh oh, that part is run mostly by your subconscious and the Super Consciousness of Creative Light and Love seems almost out of reach.

Usually we make important decisions by relying on the first stop inside, the subconscious, the ego's kingdom. Who's going to help? Ego and the evil triplets of cause. They have already shaped much of your subconscious and are ready to guide your every judgment and decision. Remember, though, using your memories and past emotional history to now guide you offers a pretty grim result. We do tend to repeat history over and over and you know how that usually turns out.

So how to change this? You will need to learn to create an open channel all the way into your Super Consciousness, for that is where the Holy Spirit and the peaceful Answer resides. This very process you have already begun practicing but we will discuss this more fully later, so be a little patient.

The path to forgiveness means seeing the whole situation differently. This seems impossible – unless, and this is important, you allow Something within you to give you a change in perspective – a new view that reframes your memories into something healing.

This cannot be an intellectual game. You cannot play at forgiveness. You cannot pretend to be forgiving. You cannot talk yourself into truly forgiving. You need to see the situation in a completely different light.

Rationalization simply won't work and means zilch if you don't actually FEEL it. And feeling it will only happen if you do one important thing. Here is comes. Be ready for it. You heard this before.

You must be willing to be wrong! Yes, be willing to be wrong about what you think happened and why you

Fast Track to Peace

think it happened and that is the key to opening the channel to the peaceful Answer, the miracle.

Being wrong is hard, but it's the only way real forgiveness can seep into your mind and replace your previous perspectives and judgments. Something wonderful, Something powerful, Something healing is deep within you trembling with anticipation, waiting for you to ask for help. That Something knows, understands and is the supreme Comforter. That Something which I have referred to as the Holy Spirit just needs to be invited in. Are you ready to take the step?

Important point

You can never forgive when you see the unforgivable as unforgivable. You will be happier if you were wrong and then the path to release can be given to you.

Fast Track to Peace

Thoughts, Suggestions, Things to Practice

1. This will take courage. Once more try practicing willingness to be wrong. Notice each time you feel you need to be right. And say to yourself, "Maybe I am not seeing the full picture here. Maybe I am wrong." You may need to practice this a lot at the beginning since it can feel really yucky.

2. When you feel ready and strong enough, take the time to explore an issue that gives you great pain. Be sure you don't wallow in the memory or you will feel excessive anger, guilt and suffering. Now, take a deep breath and ask yourself, "Maybe I am wrong. In fact, I would be a lot happier if I were wrong." Then quietly wait. You have opened a channel to a miracle.

Big Whites, Barracudas and Piranhas

At this point you have hopefully been practicing each of the previous points in each section and feel some inner changes and at least a sense of hope. Hang onto that as we continue.

You know there are dangers out there, but you swim through the waters of life and feel you have really made progress. You made lists of the areas of your life that are out of control and decided you need relief. You have acknowledged a lot of yucky feelings and actions that shamed you. You even been willing to be wrong about some of your most cherished grievances. The 'F' word (forgiveness) has entered your life and you are giving it a try. A cleansing has begun.

Fast Track to Peace

You are proud of yourself, and you should be. Here's a fun example of where you are in your progress:

You climb out of the surf, lay down on a fluffy towel and enjoy the heat of the sun and begin to doze. You feel you have earned a small vacation.

Without noticing, the tide is slowly rising. It laps gently on the shore and is soon tickling your toes. My goodness the warm water feels nice and you snooze on. Soon the water if around your knees and the tickles on your toes become more urgent, more insistent. You sit up and look at the water that is now almost around your waist and scream!

And just when you thought it was safe to be in the water - THEY'RE BACK! Guilt, fear, anger – the big whites, the barracudas and the piranhas are once more grabbing at you in the ego infested waters of life.

As Frank Sinatra sang so many years ago, "That's life". Unfortunately, or maybe fortunately, we can't learn it all, accomplish it all, release it all in one fell swoop. Layers upon layers of detritus from the depths of our subconscious, like an archeological dig, need to be slowly and carefully dug up, brushed off and examined. Most will be obvious garbage and easily thrown away. Others will be ego's

Fast Track to Peace

treasures that you can't help surreptitiously hording a little longer. Ego's evil triplets love to camouflage themselves into noble and sympathy engendering costume. They still feel comfortable for you. Aah, but are they really?

At some point you realize your subconscious is stuffed with more than you thought or wanted to recognize. But, you have come too far. You have begun noticing the peace and comfort that comes with looking into the abyss and learning there is nothing to truly fear.

But, that isn't quite enough.

Time for a deep breath. You can't hide, and you can't run. Those big whites, barracudas and piranhas are always going to be in there waiting, so the next part of the process must be taken and it's scary because it is a truly humbling experience. After all, who wants to be totally naked outside and in? Now is the time, though, when you must give it all to Someone you can't see, you are only hoping he/she is there, but who is supposed to know what to do with all your personal horrors.

No, I don't mean your friend, your sponsor, your pastor. They can be there to point you in the right direction, offer insight and especially offer support. But, now is the time for, you got, the Big Kahuna. Call him or her by any

Fast Track to Peace

name or no name, but he or she is inside of you just waiting for you to dump your stuff. Taking it all from you is the Big Kahuna's job and that Big Guy or Gal is waiting patiently for you to just let go and T R U S T.

Take that next step and trust the inner strength that waits patiently within. You got it, you must learn how to truly meditate. Now, contemplation is fine. This includes having an inner dialogue with yourself and developing loving insight, if that is what your goal is. However, meditation means you need to just stop talking - to others and to yourself. This can be truly hard. But it will bring the deepest most healing experience.

Meditation is learning to focus on the silent wellspring between thoughts, between breaths. You will just have to try this every day to understand what that means. In those small, yet immensely full slices in between what you usually focus on is the key to opening the channel to the Super Consciousness we discussed before.

Find a class, a book or a video that can guide you to learning how to access this deeply satisfying experience. This ancient process demands you learn to be silent, outside and in, and just BE. If you are already practicing, great!

Fast Track to Peace

Important point

You can't hide, and you can't run. Those big whites, barracudas and piranhas are always going to be out there waiting, so the next part of the process must be taken and it's scary, a truly humbling experience. . . .But you must do it.

Fast Track to Peace

Thoughts, Suggestions, Things to Practice

1. Divide a paper into three vertical columns. Label the first column Guilts. The second Fears. The Third Angers. These will be the painful areas of your life you want to release fully to the Holy Spirit. As the next week unfolds keep adding to each of these columns.

2. Each day find a quiet time and a quiet place to sit undisturbed. Breathe deeply with eyes closed, palms open and facing upwards on your lap. Offer each issue at a time to the Holy Spirit, moving on to the next when you feel ready to do so.

Fast Track to Peace

3. At the end of the week take the list, which may be quite long by now, to a quiet place. Here you will place the paper(s) in a firesafe container. Offer all of them at once to the Holy Spirit and set the paper(s) on fire. Watch them disappear as the smoke wafts 'heavenward'.

Looking for the Neon Sign

How did the last step go? Did you sit quietly turning your mind inward allowing that Inner Power to take your issues and give you release? Great, you are learning to go to where the truly helpful Answers reside, waiting for your requests. Silent listening each day is essential, and by now you have also noticed the pretty constant need to shift directions quickly to gain forgiving perspective as issues crop up right in front of you.

In this step we will continue to polish your practices by discussing how to recognize the Answer. Interestingly, this can sometimes be tricky. Is it from ego or from the Holy Spirit?

Let's start with a quote from *A Course in Miracles* (The last lesson in the Workbook). I love how it gives a solid starting point on how a comforting answer may come to you:

Fast Track to Peace

"This holy instant would I give to Him. . .and if I need a word to help me, He will give it to me. If I need a thought, that will He also give. And If I need but stillness and a tranquil, open mind, these are the gifts I will receive of Him. . ."

A word, a thought, or just tranquility. The answer you are looking for can come in any number of packages. And it may also happen incrementally step by step over a period of time. You may see it on a billboard, or incongruously in the middle of a news article streaming on your phone. And surprisingly of all you may find the person you consider the least helpful saying exactly what you need to hear to give you peace and release.

That last part, peace and release, will be the neon light that flashes through your mind and lifts the burdens from your heart. Here is a definition of a miracle: Something occurs that is not expected but brings great comfort.

Miracle don't fit nicely into some artificially preconceived pattern. Oh no, they come out of left field, catching you off guard making you laugh with relief and joy. Whether that miracle comes as a word, a thought or feeling of tranquility you just know all is now right with the world. You feel a sense of peace.

Just a teensy little point to remember. If you have never truly felt peace and comfort before you may not immediately notice it. You may even distrust this new experience. And for sure you will not have formed the habit of choosing peace instead of your pity party buddies of guilt, fear and anger. Rest assured you will probably still play by the old rules. The habit of choosing peace takes time and repetition.

Remember the Zen monk on the mountainside, he sits there for year upon year. And if you were to ask him if he has finished learning? He would probably say, "I am still practicing."

Important point

Rest assured you will probably still play by the old rules. The habit of choosing peace takes time and repetition.

Fast Track to Peace

Thoughts, Suggestions, Things to Practice

1. If you haven't been learning, studying and practicing a meditation technique, don't you think it's time? (The Workbook of *'A Course in Miracles'* is a great one-year course. Want some extra help? Try *'Hand in Hand – Recovery and Miracles'*, by Bette Jean Cundiff, Chapter 6, The Process of Meditation.)
2. If you are practicing meditation, great! Now, use this step to fine tune your ability to notice the Answer. Be vigilant and allow it to be truly comforting. If it's not comforting, you are editing the answer and try again.
3. Remember, keep your eyes open for miracles and allow them to change your negativity to tranquility.

Building a New Life

So, are you ready to build a peaceful life? Sounds good, right? O.K. then, the real work begins. Up to now we have been discussing, reviewing and practicing steps that can construct that peaceful life. And you have done great. You know why I can say that? Because you are reading this chapter. You have made it this far. You can be proud of yourself. Did you read every little word diligently practicing all the suggestions? Well, maybe you skipped over a word or two or slid through the practices a little too quickly. Not to worry. You have built your foundation and remember, you can always go back and study them again. But for now, let's just keep building upwards. Here are three essential building block.

Fast Track to Peace

DESIRE

To be successful at anything you first start with wanting it. Don't want it? Then trying to accomplish anything is doomed from the get go. Want peace? Then you need first to want it. I can actually hear your eyes roll around in your head as you mumble, "Well, duh!" So, let's take a teeny test.

Review the last twenty-four hours. You probably found yourself annoyed, frustrated, unhappy, irritated, righteously indignant, or something along those lines, at least once or twice. Did you in every instance immediately say to yourself, "I am not content at this moment. I must be wrong in some way. I will now ask my Inner Self to give me a new perspective." If you did that every time you felt the merest twinge of discomfort you passed the test. You desire peace.

But, if you held onto the discomfort for a while, refused to admit you might be wrong and didn't humbly ask for a new perspective, then your desire for peace was a little shaky.

First part of success - make sure you truly desire it.

Fast Track to Peace

DEDICATION

Dedication demands an internally signed contract that states you will do whatever's necessary to gain your desired goal of peace. You agree to put this goal foremost, ahead of all others.

Think about this for a moment. Peace must be more important than your pride. Peace must take precedence over monetary gain. The goal of peace must lead you through all relationship challenges, above being right and winning every discussion.

Remember, dedication is that signed contract stating your promise to make peace happen. Have you signed it? Then you are ready for the last part.

DISCIPLINE

You know you desire peace and have internally agreed with yourself to make this top priority. The work begins and continues for the rest of your life. You can no longer have a vacation from the goal of peace.

Every day you must wake up with a prayer for peace in your mind and on your lips.

Fast Track to Peace

Every day you must monitor your emotional responses to life with greater and deeper insight, being truthful and not deceptive in your interpretations.

Every day you send yourself off to sleep with gratitude for the miracles you have been given. And you will notice them more and more as you become adept at being a peaceful person.

You desire peace.

You signed a contract dedicating yourself to the process.

You are practicing every day. Miracles of healing, joy and peace are yours.

The directions are simple but powerfully effective when you just do it!

Important point

*The work begins and continues
for the rest of your life.*

Fast Track to Peace

Thoughts, Suggestions, Things to Practice

1. Look back at your life's journey and notice those times when you deeply wanted something but never accomplished getting it? Review what happened to create failure and notice where the breakdown occurred - in your desire, your dedication or your discipline to attaining your goal.

2. Once more look back at your life's journey and notice those times when you deeply wanted something and accomplished getting it. Review what happened to create success. Notice your level of desire, your dedication and your disciplined effort and how they each alone and together carried you to the goal.

Fast Track to Peace

One more thing. . .

Fast Track to Peace

Just one rule!

That's all we are asked to follow in this lifetime. Just one simple rule, "...to be truly helpful." (*A Course in Miracles*)

Ah, but helpfulness, what does that really mean? And what does it look like? The answer like the rule, is ridiculously simple - help each person we meet (or even think of), lift the crushing and relentless sense of unworthiness from their shoulders. In other words, allow the experience of our shared, innate, spiritual innocence to fill both our minds and the peace this brings, together.

Now, there are many ways to remove debilitating guilt that leads to fear and calls for action, or in other words anger. What gets a little tricky is that anyone swept up by the evil triplets is in a precarious emotional whirlpool. Logic rarely reaches into that vortex. Ego has its own reasoning to fit each of its beloved offspring. Approaching

Fast Track to Peace

with calm rational, carefully built arguments for peace and release will be rebuffed. The degree to which ego has its strangle hold on the other's emotions will probably determine the degree to which your 'helpful' suggestions are met with armed resistance – a nasty look, a comment like, "You just can't understand!", to a screamed rant that could last awhile, or actual fisticuffs.

Note: when you step in to challenge another's judgments and emotional responses you are perceived as saying, "Look dummy, you are wrong, but I am smarter and know better than you so just do it my way." Their ego's response to this will be to dig deep and prove the smartness of its own logic and show you how stupid you are.

Now is the time to turn the other proverbial cheek and not retaliate. By the way let's get something clear. Turning the other cheek doesn't mean allowing yourself to get beaten up physically, verbally or emotionally again and again. Instead, when you allow the Holy Spirit to show you again and again another's worth and desperate call for help, the whole dynamic changes radically. Ask within and you will be told by Inner Wisdom what to do and say for

Fast Track to Peace

exactly in that particular moment resulting in release for both of you.

This is why when I have often been asked, "Can't I confront someone and get them to think differently?" My answer is this: Be absolutely sure that the person you are confronting is a 'walk on water realized master'. He or she will see your efforts as an offer of help and appreciate your efforts. But, should this person not quite have reached that level of spiritual accomplishment, he or she will probably see your efforts as an attack, and retaliation will follow.

So, what can you do? First be sure your own motives for helping are 'pure', or in other words you just want to help and not use this as an opportunity to show how cool you are. This takes honest assessment of yourself!

Next, ask for guidance. Yes. Take this moment to ask within for help. The word or thought or need for silence will come as an answer. Helping someone will always help you also. The result? You will be healed together. Being free of guilt, fear, and anger brings overwhelming joy. This is the definition of healing.

"To heal is to make joyful," a line from *A Course in Miracles,* offers us a great proactive position. Don't take

Fast Track to Peace

everything and everyone so seriously. Instead see the gentle humor in the world and share this with others.

This is important! Don't belittle others with a mistaken belief that it's humor! Sarcasm is one of ego's sharp weapons. Instead laugh with the sheer joy of life and other can't help laughing joyfully with you.

We have just one little rule – to be truly helpful – to lift debilitating fear, guilt and its coping tactic called anger from the whole world. Whew! Then after that, what's left but world peace! Cool? Sure, but that means we must stop finding fault with those who are not yet willing to give up that deliciously, self-sabotaging sense of unworthiness and the need to project it in anger onto others, which is called by the way, war. Instead of war, we need to share a good laugh.

O.K. Then our job is to take just one little step at a time, one little thought at a time, with just a little bit of willingness to rip away the old patterns and choose peace. We must be willing to be wrong and we need to open our mind to the Holy Spirit to allow Him to replace fear, guilt and anger with a radiant new perspective. We will be healed as we let Inner Wisdom show us how to joyfully see the world and bring that joy to the world - one encounter at a time.

Important point

Don't take everything and everyone so seriously. Instead see the gentle humor in the world and share this with others.

Something to consider:

1. Here is prayer from '*A Course in Miracles*' that I and so many have memorized. Try doing the same. These words can help you when you are confused and uncertain, and others around you are desperately calling for help.

    (I have changed a word or two and added a few, but you can find the exact wording in Chapter 2 of the Text, 'A Course in Miracles'.)

Fast Track to Peace

I am here only to be truly helpful.

I am here to represent (You) who sent me.

I do not have to worry about what to say or what to do because (You) who sent me will direct me.

I am content to be wherever (You) wish knowing (You) go there with me.

I will be healed as I let (You) teach me to heal (myself and others through forgiveness)

A Last Personal Note

Thank you for studying this material. Why am I thanking you? Because with each peaceful thought a wave of gentleness and healing enters the whole Universe to cleanse and bless everyone and everything.

So, again thank you. You have helped heal others, including me, as you have learned to heal yourself.

Bette Jean Cundiff

Made in the USA
Las Vegas, NV
16 June 2022